EARTH AND ITS MOON

the solar system

EARTH AND ITS MOON

Edited by Michael Anderson

Britannica®
Educational Publishing

IN ASSOCIATION WITH

ROSEN
EDUCATIONAL SERVICES

Published in 2012 by Britannica Educational Publishing
(a trademark of Encyclopædia Britannica, Inc.)
in association with Rosen Educational Services, LLC
29 East 21st Street, New York, NY 10010.

Distributed exclusively by Rosen Educational Services.
For a listing of additional Britannica Educational Publishing titles, call toll free (800) 237-9932.

First Edition

Britannica Educational Publishing
Michael I. Levy: Executive Editor, Encyclopædia Britannica
J.E. Luebering: Director, Core Reference Group, Encyclopædia Britannica
Adam Augustyn: Assistant Manager, Encyclopædia Britannica

Anthony L. Green: Editor, Compton's by Britannica
Michael Anderson: Senior Editor, Compton's by Britannica
Sherman Hollar: Associate Editor, Compton's by Britannica

Marilyn L. Barton: Senior Coordinator, Production Control
Steven Bosco: Director, Editorial Technologies
Lisa S. Braucher: Senior Producer and Data Editor
Yvette Charboneau: Senior Copy Editor
Kathy Nakamura: Manager, Media Acquisition

Rosen Educational Services
Jeanne Nagle: Senior Editor
Nelson Sá: Art Director
Cindy Reiman: Photography Manager
Matthew Cauli: Designer, Cover Design
Introduction by Jeanne Nagle

Library of Congress Cataloging-in-Publication Data

Earth and its moon / edited by Michael Anderson.
       p. cm. — (The solar system)
"In association with Britannica Educational Publishing, Rosen Educational Services."
Includes bibliographical references and index.
ISBN 978-1-61530-515-5 (library binding)
1. Earth—Juvenile literature. 2. Moon—Juvenile literature. I. Anderson, Michael, 1972-
QB631.4.E28 2012
525—dc22
                                                                                    2011002175

Manufactured in the United States of America

CONTENTS

Long ago, Earth was the subject of great speculation. Ancient astronomers such as Ptolemy thought that Earth was the center of the universe. Likewise, there have been all sorts of assumptions about Earth's satellite, the Moon. One of the most interesting beliefs was that moonlight was capable of driving a person crazy.

Using a telescope, Galileo Galilei went on to show that the Sun was actually the center of the universe. And while some folks still believe that a full Moon brings out the "weird" in people, they have plenty of solid evidence that proves the Moon has real natural effects on Earth. For instance, the gravitational pull of the Moon during its many phases influences ocean tides. Many additional facts about Earth and the Moon have been discovered over the years. The results of years of research into the nature of Earth and the Moon are the subject of this book.

More is known about Earth than any other planet in the solar system, mainly because scientists have had the advantage of living here. Even before the advent of helpful technology such as the telescope and computers, scientists managed to find ways to figure out certain characteristics of the planet. These included its size, shape, and movement. For instance, ancient Egyptians measured shadow length and factored in the distance between cities to obtain a rough estimate of Earth's circumference.

To find out about Earth's physical structure, scientists test and observe the planet's surface layer, known as the crust. Using material from this and the top of the next deepest layer, the mantle, they can work out formulas that tell them what's happening all the way down to Earth's center, the core. To study the atmosphere—the envelope of gases surrounding Earth—scientists have an array of other techniques and tools, including radar and tethered balloons that carry sophisticated instruments.

Manned space missions have provided scientists with plenty of information about the Moon's physical characteristics. Testing of Moon rocks revealed the age and composition of the satellite's surface. Long before the rocket age, ancient astronomers used math, observation, and simple deduction to guesstimate measurements of the Moon's size and its distance from Earth.

Exploration, observation, and experimentation have answered many questions, and dispelled many myths, concerning Earth and its satellite. Yet there are still many mysteries to be solved regarding this ever-evolving planet and its moon.

1 chapter

PLANET EARTH

The third planet from the Sun is Earth, the home of all known life. While it shares many characteristics with other planets, its physical properties and history allow it to support life in its near-surface environment. Liquid water, which is essential for all known forms of life, is found in abundance on Earth. Deep, salty oceans cover more than two thirds of the surface.

In addition, Earth's oxygen-rich atmosphere is unique. This characteristic is actually not surprising, however, since large amounts of oxygen exist in the atmosphere only because living things constantly supply it. Earth's green plants take in carbon dioxide and give off oxygen, which humans and other animals need to breathe. This is one example of how life itself has altered the planet in ways that generally help maintain the conditions for life. Scientists have come to view Earth as a dynamic world with many interacting systems. Understanding these relationships will surely be important as human activities increasingly affect the planet's surface, oceans, and atmosphere.

SHAPE AND SIZE

Many ancient cultures, even sophisticated ones such as the Egyptians, pictured Earth as being flat, with the sky above being a separate abode of heavenly bodies: the Sun, Moon, planets, and stars. By 2500 BC, though, some people correctly thought Earth to be roughly spherical in shape. The Greek mathematician Pythagoras is widely credited with reaching this conclusion in the 6th century BC. Two centuries later, Aristotle gave specific reasons for thinking Earth is round: (1) matter is drawn to Earth's center and would naturally compress it into a spherical shape, (2) traveling south reveals new stars rising above

Astronauts aboard the Apollo 17 spacecraft captured a stunning image of Earth as the spacecraft headed to the Moon in 1972. Vast oceans and seas surround the continent of Africa, the island of Madagascar, and, at top, the Arabian Peninsula. Also visible are clouds in the atmosphere and the south polar ice cap. **NASA**

the southern horizon, and (3) Earth's shadow on the Moon at lunar eclipses is circular.

After Aristotle, many people did not know about his teachings. Belief in a flat Earth could persist, and there was at least some debate on the issue. However, knowledge of the spherical shape of Earth has been widespread among astronomers for most of the last 2,000 years, at least. Greek and Indian astronomers accepted the concept, and by the 9th century AD Islamic astronomers were using it. Christian Europe had widely accepted the idea by the 13th century.

The field of measurement of Earth is called geodesy. One of the earliest known attempts to calculate the circumference of Earth was that of Eratosthenes, a librarian at the library of Alexandria in Egypt, in about 250 BC. He knew that at about noon on the day of the summer solstice (the day the noon Sun was highest in the sky), a vertical stick in Alexandria would cast a shadow that made an angle of about 7 degrees with the stick. He also knew that in Syene (now Aswan), Egypt, the Sun would pass directly overhead on that day, shining to the bottom of a deep well. By using an estimate of the north-south distance between the two cities, and assuming that the Sun was very far away, he was able to calculate

Earth's circumference within a relatively small percentage of the value now known.

It is now known that the circumference at the Equator is 24,902 miles (40,075 kilometers). The diameter at the Equator is 7,926 miles (12,756 kilometers). Actually, Earth is not quite spherical but is an oblate spheroid — squashed in the north-south direction so that the pole-to-pole diameter is only 7,900 miles (12,714 kilometers). The distance from the Equator to the North Pole along Earth's

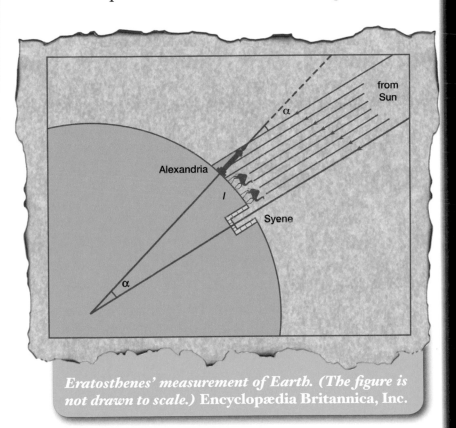

Eratosthenes' measurement of Earth. (The figure is not drawn to scale.) **Encyclopædia Britannica, Inc.**

surface is 6,214 miles (10,002 kilometers). In fact, the meter was originally defined (by the French Academy of Sciences in 1791) to be one ten-millionth of the distance from the Equator to the North Pole. This explains why this distance is almost exactly 10 million meters (10,000 kilometers).

MOTIONS

For centuries Earth was simply "the world" — the only one known. Even most believers in a spherical Earth thought it to be a one-of-a-kind object in the center of a spherical universe. The Sun, Moon, planets, and stars were generally thought to be of a very different nature from Earth. In fact, in the 4th century BC Aristotle proposed that they were made of a heavenly fifth element that he called "quintessence." This was in addition to his supposed earthly elements of earth, water, air, and fire. The Sun and Moon, plus Mercury, Venus, Mars, Jupiter, and Saturn (all easily visible to the naked eye), were seen to gradually change position relative to the stars. This earned them the name planets, which meant "wanderers."

Most thinkers, including Aristotle, believed that Earth was motionless in the center of the universe. This is called the geocentric (Earth-centered) theory, and it was developed in greater detail by Ptolemy of Alexandria in around AD 150. Almost all astronomers accepted the theory for the next 1,400 years. In this view, Earth was certainly not a planet because it was obviously not a wandering light in the sky.

ROTATION AND ORBIT

In the 16th century AD Nicholas Copernicus of Poland proposed that Earth rotates on an axis through the North and South poles once a day—actually once a "sidereal" day, which is measured using the distant stars as a reference frame instead of the Sun. Earth's sidereal day is 23 hours, 56 minutes, and 4 seconds, which is a few minutes shorter than its "solar" day. Copernicus also said that Earth orbits, or revolves around, the Sun once a sidereal year (which is 365.256 days). He believed that the Moon orbits Earth but that the other wanderers (the planets, not including the Sun) revolve around the Sun like Earth does. In this, Earth is a planet, because it, too, is a wanderer—around the Sun.

Copernicus' heliocentric (Sun-centered) theory was slow to be accepted. However,

Johannes Kepler of Germany assumed this basic view in developing his three laws of planetary motion in the early 17th century. One of these laws states that a planet's orbit, or path around the Sun, is an ellipse, with the Sun not at the exact center but at one of two points called foci. Earth's orbit turns out to be more nearly a circle than the orbits of most of the other planets. Earth's distance from the Sun varies by only a small percentage, from about 91.4 million miles (147.1 million kilometers) in early January to some 94.5 million miles (152.1 million kilometers) in early July.

THE EFFECT OF GRAVITY

In 1687 Isaac Newton of England published his law of universal gravitation in his major work, the *Principia*. This explained the planets' motions as being caused by the Sun's gravitational pull on the planets. By this point, almost all scientists accepted the heliocentric theory.

Newton showed that any two objects attract each other with this gravitational force. Its strength is proportional to the mass of each object, and it becomes weaker with increasing distance between the objects.

GRAVITATION

The force that causes objects to drop and water to run downhill is the same force that holds the Earth, the Sun, and the stars together and keeps the Moon and artificial satellites in their orbits. Gravitation, the attraction of all matter for all other matter, is both the most familiar of the natural forces and the least understood.

Gravity is the weakest of the four forces that are currently known to govern the way physical objects behave. The other three forces are electromagnetism, which governs such familiar phenomena as electricity and magnetism; the "strong force," which is responsible for the events in nuclear reactors and hydrogen bombs; and the "weak force," which is involved with radioactivity. Because of its weakness, gravity is difficult to study in the laboratory.

Despite its weakness, gravitation is important because, unlike the other three forces, it is universally attractive and also acts over an infinite distance. Over distances ranging from those measurable on Earth to those in the farthest parts of the universe, gravitational attraction is a significant force and, in many cases, the dominant one.

Both Sir Isaac Newton in the 17th century and Albert Einstein in the 20th century initiated revolutions in the study and observation of the universe through new theories of gravity. The subject is today at the forefront of theoretical physics and astronomy.

A body's "weight" is simply the gravitational force exerted on it by Earth or whatever planet or other large body it happens to be near. Objects naturally tend to fly off through space in a straight line at a constant speed, but a gravitational pull can curve the path into a closed orbit. The Moon orbits Earth, and likewise Earth orbits the Sun.

SOLSTICES AND EQUINOXES

Earth's spin axis is tilted about 23.5 degrees with respect to the axis of its revolution around the Sun. This allows the Northern Hemisphere to get the most sunlight—and therefore its summer—on about June 21, when the North Pole is tipped toward the Sun. The North Pole points almost the same direction all year, toward the North Star. On about December 21 Earth is on the opposite side of the Sun, though, so the South Pole is tipped toward the Sun and the Southern Hemisphere gets the most sunshine and its summer at that time. These dates are called the solstices. The equinoxes, when day and night are of nearly equal length worldwide, occur in between, on around March 21 and September 23. Thus the seasons are controlled much more by the tilt of Earth's axis than by the rather small variation in distance from the Sun.

The spin axis itself wobbles, much like that of a top, slowly over time. This is the main cause of the "precession of the equinoxes," a roughly 26,000-year cycle in which the spin axis traces out a circle, 47 degrees wide, in the sky. On this circle lie several "candidates" for North Star. Polaris is the present North Star, since currently Earth's axis points almost directly at it. Some 13,000 years from now, though, the North Star will be the bright star Vega. The Greek astronomer Hipparchus recognized this subtle phenomenon in the 2nd century BC.

MAGNETIC FIELD

Hundreds of years ago, the Chinese discovered a curious property of certain metallic rocks. If floated on a piece of wood in water, such rocks (or similarly magnetized iron needles) would rotate into a specific orientation relative to north and south. These rocks also had the ability to attract bits of iron. This was the discovery of magnetism (and the invention of the compass) and also that Earth itself is a giant magnet.

This invisible effect is now described as due to a magnetic field, a region of influence around any magnet. Earth has north and south magnetic poles that are near, but not quite on, the actual geographic North and South poles. The planet's magnetic field can be illustrated by lines, called magnetic field lines, that connect the magnetic poles and curve out and around the edges of the field, forming closed loops. Scientists believe that Earth's magnetic field is generated by huge currents of molten metal flowing in the liquid outer core.

Earth's magnetic field has far more important effects than just deflecting compass needles. It shields Earth by steering and trapping electrically charged particles, such as protons and electrons, ejected by the Sun. This stream of particles is called the solar wind. The particles in it travel about 1 million miles (1.6 million kilometers) per hour, reaching Earth in a few days. Once trapped, the particles travel in a corkscrew pattern and effectively bounce back and forth between the poles.

The region of space in which Earth's magnetic field dominates the environment and traps particles from the solar wind is called the magnetosphere. Many of the charged particles remain trapped there. The greatest concentrations of these particles are in two regions called the Van Allen radiation belts, located mainly between 5,000 and 20,000 miles (8,000 and 32,000 kilometers) above the ground.

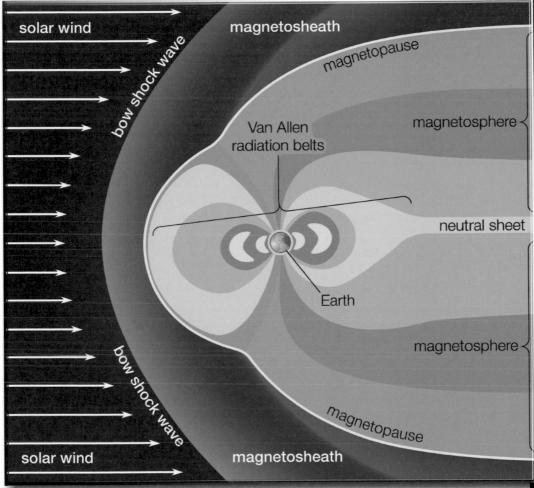

Within Earth's magnetosphere (shown in cross section) are the Van Allen radiation belts, regions with high concentrations of electrically charged particles. Pressure from the solar wind is responsible for the asymmetrical shape of the magnetosphere and the belts. **Encyclopædia Britannica, Inc.**

If the magnetic field did not prevent many of the solar wind particles from striking the atmosphere, the solar wind might gradually erode away much of the planet's atmosphere. Mars, which is almost devoid of a magnetic field, has an atmosphere only about one hundredth as dense as Earth's. Mars's weaker gravity would probably have left it with less of an atmosphere anyway, but its exposure to the solar wind very likely helped remove some of its air.

The solar system consists of the Sun and all the objects that orbit it, including Earth. (The drawing is not to scale overall.) **Encyclopædia Britannica, Inc.**

Solar System
The distance between each object and the Sun is shown in astronomical units (AU). One AU equals the average distance from Earth to the Sun. It is about 93 million miles (150 million kilometers).

inner planets are shown in scale to each other

Earth
1 AU

Venus
0.7 AU

Moon

Mercury
0.4 AU

Mars
1.5 AU

asteroid belt
2 to 4.5 AU

Sun

Kuiper belt
30 to 50 AU

Jupiter
5.2 AU

EARTH'S PLACE IN SPACE

As originally proposed, the heliocentric theory held that the Sun was stationary. In the last hundred years or so, the perspective on this has changed dramatically. It turns out that the stars are actually other suns (so the Sun is a star), all of which move through space. Moreover, many of them may have planets of their own. The first extrasolar planet was discovered in 1995. Within 15 years, more than 200 more such planets were discovered, mainly using indirect

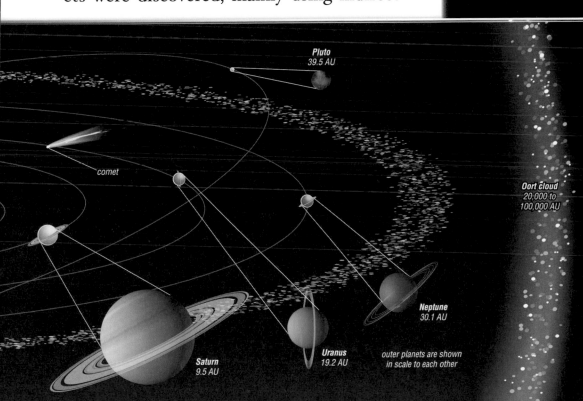

comet

Pluto
39.5 AU

Oort Cloud
20,000 to
100,000 AU

Neptune
30.1 AU

Uranus
19.2 AU

outer planets are shown
in scale to each other

Saturn
9.5 AU

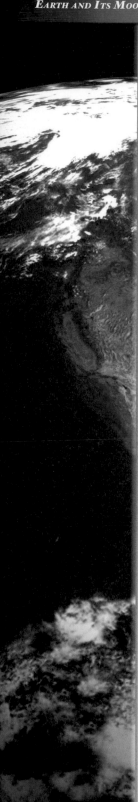

methods such as analyzing the slight wobble of the parent star in response to the planet's gravitational tug on it.

The nearest star system is about 270,000 times as far from Earth as the Sun is. Most of the stars visible to the naked eye are over a million times as far as the Sun, thus explaining why they appear so faint. Many would appear much brighter than the Sun if placed where the Sun is. All the stars one can see with the naked eye are nearby neighbors in a gigantic disklike structure called the Milky Way galaxy, which contains over a hundred billion suns.

The Sun ("our" Sun) is about 27,000 light-years from the center of the Milky Way. A light-year is the distance light travels in a year, almost 6 trillion miles (9.5 trillion kilometers). The Sun and its planets orbit the Milky Way's center with a period (the time it takes to complete one orbit) of about 250 million years. The Milky Way, in turn, is only one of billions of galaxies in the observable universe. The galaxies are generally flying apart from each other and are scattered across billions of light-years of space.

THE STRUCTURE OF EARTH

The parts of Earth that people can see—the land and the oceans—have long been the subject of intensive research by scientists. The great bulk of the planet, however, lies beyond the reach of direct observation. Nevertheless, using indirect methods, scientists have been able to determine what lies beneath Earth's surface.

DISCOVERING EARTH'S STRUCTURE

To know what Earth is like inside, one might imagine drilling all the way to the center. Nothing anywhere near close to this has ever been done, though. The deepest well, on the Kola Peninsula in Russia, is about 7.6 miles (12.3 kilometers) deep, reaching only about $\frac{1}{500}$ the distance to Earth's center. The question remains, then, how can humans discover the structure of the planet?

While scientists have almost literally "barely scratched the surface" of Earth, a great deal has been learned about Earth's interior. One approach is to consider Earth's

average density and the density and chemical composition of the near-surface layers, including rocks conveniently brought to the surface by volcanoes. Another method is to study the vibrations called seismic waves, which travel through the planet after being produced by natural sources such as earthquakes and by manmade events such as nuclear weapons tests.

USING DENSITY

Earth's mass is known from its gravitational effects to be 5.976×10^{24} kilograms, which if it could be weighed on another "Earth," would amount to about 6.587 billion trillion tons. Combined with knowledge of Earth's volume, this gives a density of 5.52 grams per cubic centimeter. This is denser than the typical 2 to 3 grams per cubic centimeter for rocks but less than the densities of iron and nickel, which are about 8 and 9 grams per cubic centimeter, respectively. These metals are commonly found in meteorites and may have been much of the raw material for Earth. Therefore, one might suppose Earth to be some mixture of rock and metal. Furthermore, iron and nickel, being denser than rock, would tend to sink toward the center.

USING SEISMIC WAVES

When Earth is disturbed by an earthquake, several kinds of waves are produced, all of which can be recorded by instruments called seismometers. Some of these waves travel along Earth's surface. Rayleigh waves are much like the rolling waves on the ocean surface. Love waves vibrate side-to-side, for example, east-to-west for a northward traveling wave. Together, these waves produce most of the damage to buildings during earthquakes.

Other waves travel downward into Earth's interior. These waves

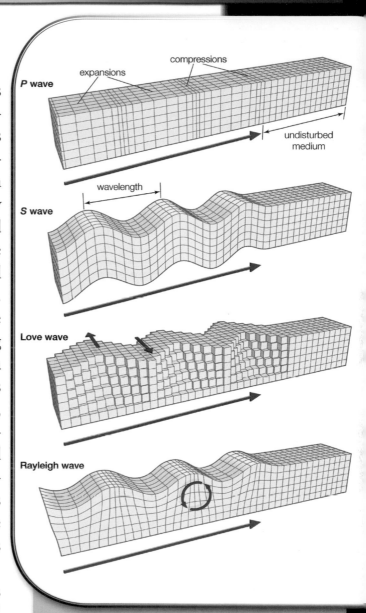

The main types of seismic waves are P, S, Love, and Rayleigh. Encyclopædia Britannica, Inc.

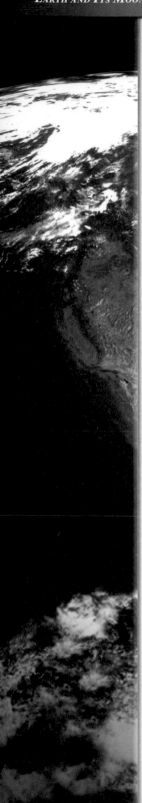

are known as body waves, and they come in two basic types. *P*, or primary, waves have a "push-pull" motion parallel to the direction the wave is traveling. *S*, or secondary, waves make a side-to-side motion, perpendicular to the direction of wave motion. The *P* waves travel faster, hence the name primary, since they arrive first. Both types of waves generally travel faster in denser material. This not only affects arrival time but also allows the waves to bend (refract) and bounce (reflect) upon encountering changes in the density of the material. *S* waves have the additional property of not being able to travel through liquids.

By carefully analyzing data from thousands of earthquakes, using seismometers scattered across the globe, scientists have developed a rather detailed picture of Earth's interior. This technique is called seismic tomography. It is similar to the use of ultrasonic sound waves to produce images of unborn babies or computed tomography (CT) X-ray scans for diagnosing medical conditions.

A very notable result is that something inside the planet casts "shadows" for *S* waves on the side of Earth opposite a given earthquake. In other words, these waves are absent on the opposite side. *S* waves do not travel through liquid, but *P* waves do. Since *S* waves cannot travel through liquid, this indicates the existence of a large liquid layer deep inside Earth. *P* waves can travel through it, and the arrival times and refractions of these waves show that there is a solid core inside this liquid layer. (See diagram on this page.)

Seismic tomography also readily yields details of the outer layers of the planet. The outermost part, the crust, has rather low density rock in which waves travel somewhat slowly. The waves partially reflect upon reaching a boundary, called the Moho. This is short for the Mohorovičić discontinuity, named after

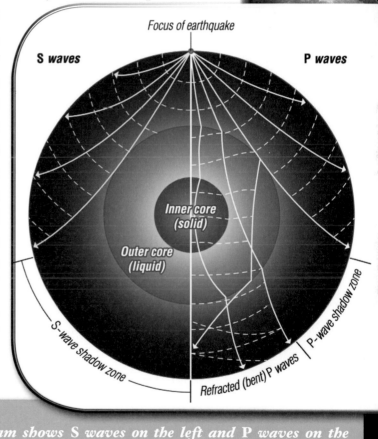

A simplified diagram shows S waves on the left and P waves on the right, but waves of both types would actually radiate in all directions. Encyclopædia Britannica, Inc.

Andrija Mohorovičić , the Croatian seismologist who discovered it in 1909. The depth at which this discontinuity occurs ranges from as little as 3 miles (5 kilometers) beneath some parts of the ocean bottom to up to about 45 miles (75 kilometers) beneath some continental surfaces.

EARTH'S LAYERS

The picture, then, is as follows. Earth's outermost layer, the crust, consists of solid rock. The crust of the continents is thicker and less dense than that of the ocean bottom. The Moho marks the boundary between the crust and the denser rock of the layer beneath it, the mantle, which contains over half the planet's mass. The crust and outermost mantle together are called the lithosphere, from the Greek word *lithos*, meaning "rock."

Temperatures and pressures rise with increasing depth inside the planet. At roughly 50 miles (80 kilometers) below the surface, the rock of the mantle is at about 2,500 °F (1,370 °C) and becomes partly molten. This is the beginning of the part of the mantle known as the asthenosphere. Below about 150 to 200 miles (250 to 300 kilometers), the mantle is under so much pressure that it becomes more rigid again, though it is still plastic enough to allow very gradual motions. The mantle extends down to about 1,800 miles (2,900 kilometers) beneath the surface. The temperature at the bottom of the mantle is believed to be roughly 6,700 °F (3,700 °C).

Beneath the mantle, the material becomes much denser (as indicated by faster P waves) and liquefies (as evidenced by the lack of S waves). Scientists believe that this layer, called the outer core, consists of up to 90 percent molten iron

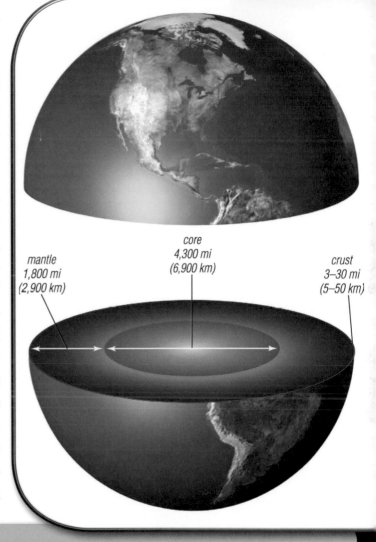

mantle
1,800 mi
(2,900 km)

core
4,300 mi
(6,900 km)

crust
3–30 mi
(5–50 km)

Earth's interior has three main layers: a thin, rocky crust; a thick, rocky mantle; and a metallic core. The measurements provided are averages.
Encyclopædia Britannica, Inc.

and nickel (mostly iron), with some other elements such as sulfur mixed in. It makes up about 30 percent of Earth's mass. Finally, below about 3,200 miles (5,100 kilometers)

Earth's Outer Layers

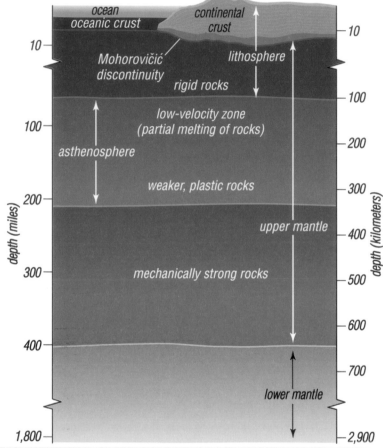

A cross section shows Earth's outer layers subdivided according to their physical properties. The crust and the uppermost part of the mantle form the rigid lithosphere. Below that is a partly molten zone, which overlies a more rigid zone. Encyclopædia Britannica, Inc.

is the inner core, which extends to the very center, about 3,960 miles (6,370 kilometers) down. It contains about 2 percent of Earth's mass. Despite extremely high temperatures, estimated to be between 8,000 and 12,000 °F (about 4,400 and 6,600 °C), the pressure is so high that the iron and nickel become solid.

ROCKS AND MINERALS

Earth is largely a ball of rock. Rocks form on and beneath Earth's surface under a wide range of physical and chemical conditions.

All rocks are made up of minerals. The minerals in some rocks are single chemical elements such as gold or copper, but the minerals in most rocks are compounds— combinations of elements with a definite chemical composition and a precisely patterned structure. Most minerals form crystals. Each crystal has a characteristic shape and structure that is determined by the type and arrangement of its atoms.

The most common atoms present in Earth's rocks are oxygen and silicon, which combine to make silicates such as quartz (SiO_2). Silicates make up about 95 percent of the planet's crust and upper mantle. Other common elements, present in lesser

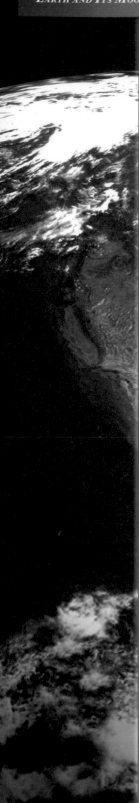

amounts, are aluminum, iron, calcium, sodium, potassium, and magnesium.

IGNEOUS ROCK

Igneous rock is the primary rock of Earth's crust in that most other kinds of rock found on Earth form from it. Igneous rock is rock that solidifies from a molten state. The molten rock material under Earth's surface is called magma. Magma that is forced out onto Earth's surface, onto either the ocean bottom or the land, as in volcanic action, is called lava.

Magma deep beneath the surface may cool slowly. When this happens, the minerals grow slowly and may reach a relatively large size. This slow-cooling process produces coarse-grained rocks such as granite or gabbro. The type of rock produced depends on the chemicals in the magma. Each type can be distinguished by its characteristic mineral composition.

Magma closer to the surface cools more quickly, giving the minerals little chance to grow. As a result, fine-grained rocks similar in composition to the coarse-grained ones are produced. The fine-grained rhyolite is the equivalent of the coarse-grained granite, and the fine-grained basalt is the equivalent of gabbro.

Some materials ejected from volcanoes cool so quickly that they solidify before they strike the ground. Lava cools so rapidly that often gas bubbles are trapped within it. When such lava hardens, it is light and porous. Pumice is formed in this way. The natural glass obsidian is also formed from lava.

METAMORPHIC ROCK

Metamorphic rock results when heat and pressure change the

Towering columns of basalt, an igneous rock, make up the unusual formation known as the Devils Postpile, part of a national monument in east-central California. It formed within the last 100,000 years, when a lava flow filled a valley floor and then very slowly cooled and cracked into many-sided columns. Glaciers later eroded most of the hardened lava, revealing the sides of the remaining columns. **Kirkendall/Spring**

original composition and structure of rock. The original rock may be of any type—igneous, sedimentary, or other metamorphic rock. Deep in Earth's crust the temperature is much higher than it is near the surface, and the hot rock is subjected to pressure from the weight of the crust above and from lateral movements of the crust. Sometimes liquids and gases also act on the rock to change it.

Limestone, a sedimentary rock, changes to marble as a result of such forces. Under stress, the mineral grains in the sedimentary rock shale grow in new directions to form slate, a metamorphic rock. Continued stress changes the slate to phyllite and then to schist, a rock that is very different in appearance, composition, and structure from the original shale. Quartzite, one of the hardest and most compact rocks, is the metamorphic form of the relatively soft, grainy sandstone, a sedimentary rock.

Sedimentary Rock

Sedimentary rocks form at or near Earth's surface, often through the weathering action of wind and running water. In fact, rocks of this type cover much of the surface, but they are often hidden by a thin layer of soil. For

The erosion of sandstone created spectacular formations in Arizona. A sedimentary rock, sandstone consists of grains of sand that have been cemented or compressed into rock. Jeremy Woodhouse/Getty Images

convenience, sedimentary rocks are divided into two major groups: clastic rocks and crystalline rocks. Clastic rocks are composed of sediment—particles or fragments of rock—of varying sizes that have been compacted or cemented together. Crystalline rocks are composed of minerals that have been precipitated out of solutions.

Particles of rock, eroded from exposed areas such as mountains, are transported by streams and rivers to the sea. There they slowly settle as fine silts or clays. Coarser particles, such as sands, are deposited nearer the shore, and the largest particles, such as pebbles and cobbles, settle at the shoreline.

THE SIGNIFICANCE OF SEDIMENTARY ROCKS

Mineral resources such as coal, petroleum, and natural gas occur in sedimentary rocks. In addition, geologists can reconstruct the ancient geography and environment of a region by studying the distribution of its sedimentary rocks, which lie in layers, or strata. Correlating the sequences of rock layers in different areas enables them to trace a particular geologic event to a particular period.

Fossils help geologists establish the relative geologic ages of layers of rock. In this diagram, sections A and B represent rock layers 200 miles (300 kilometers) apart. Their respective ages can be established by means of the fossils in each layer. **Encyclopædia Britannica, Inc.**

Fossils—the remains, imprints, or traces of organisms that once lived on Earth—are found almost exclusively in sedimentary rocks. They record the history of life on Earth, though only certain parts of a small percentage of ancient life, most often the solid skeleton or shell of animals with such parts or the woody structures of certain plants, are preserved as fossils. In unusual circumstances, the soft tissues of living things have been preserved.

As these materials slowly accumulate over long periods of time, water is squeezed out from between the particles. Cementing agents carried in solution in the water—for example, calcium carbonate, silica, and iron oxide—may bind the particles together.

The pebbles close to shore are cemented together into a conglomerate. A little farther out shales form. In the open oceans limestones form from calcium carbonate and the shells of dead sea animals.

Crystalline rocks can form in shallow inland seas where access to open water has been restricted or cut off. In such places the seas may evaporate slowly, leaving behind compounds that form sedimentary rocks such as gypsum and rock salt.

EARTH'S SPHERES

One approach to understanding Earth, especially the outer parts, is to divide it into interacting spheres. One such scheme considers these to be the atmosphere, the hydrosphere, the lithosphere, and the biosphere.

ATMOSPHERE

The atmosphere is the envelope of gases surrounding the planet. It clings to Earth because, having mass, it is gravitationally attracted to the mass of the rest of the planet. Gas molecules move quite rapidly at earthly temperatures, and a few of them actually escape into space.

Fortunately, Earth's atmosphere is massive enough so that this leakage has not caused a significant loss of its gases over the billions of years scientists believe it has existed. Smaller worlds, such as the Moon and Mars, have not been so successful at holding onto any air they might have ever had. The Moon has virtually no atmosphere, and that of Mars is much thinner (less dense) than Earth's.

MASS AND COMPOSITION

The atmosphere's mass is just over 5×10^{18} kilograms (5 million gigatons, with a gigaton equaling a billion metric tons), which weighs more than 11×10^{18} pounds. This may sound impressive, but it is less than one millionth the mass of the whole planet. Traces of the atmosphere can be found 100 miles (160 kilometers) above the surface, but most of it lies within 3.5 miles (5.6 kilometers) of the

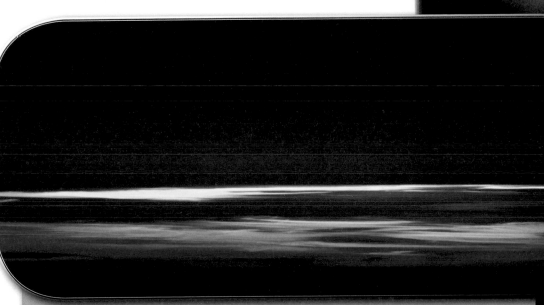

Luminous layers of the atmosphere appear above the dark edge of Earth, at bottom, in an image captured at sunset by astronauts aboard the International Space Station. The orange and red layer is the lowest and densest layer of the atmosphere, called the troposphere, while the blue layer is the stratosphere. **Courtesy, Image Science & Analysis Laboratory, NASA Johnson Space Center, No. ISS001-421-24**

ground. On the scale of a typical globe with a 12-inch (30-centimeter) diameter, this is little more than the thickness of a sheet of paper.

About 78 percent by volume of dry air consists of nitrogen (chemical formula N_2). Oxygen (O_2) makes up 21 percent. Most of the rest is argon (Ar), but small amounts of other gases, such as carbon dioxide (CO_2), methane (CH_4), and hydrogen (H_2), are present as well. Notice that these figures are for dry air; water vapor (H_2O) makes up varying amounts, usually between 0.1 and 4 percent.

The composition of the air is very nearly uniform across the globe and even at different heights. However, a small (a few parts per million) concentration of ozone (O_3) exists in the layer called the stratosphere, mostly more than about 6 miles (10 kilometers) above the ground. This "ozone layer" is vital to life on Earth because it absorbs most of the harmful ultraviolet rays reaching Earth from the Sun. This concentration of ozone has been reduced in recent decades, at least in part because of reactions with man-made chemical compounds called chlorofluorocarbons (CFCs), used in commerce and industry. Since 1992, production of these gases has been greatly restricted, so it is hoped that little further damage to the ozone layer will occur.

TEMPERATURE AND PRESSURE

Though composition changes only slightly with height, the temperature and pressure of the air vary greatly. In the lower part of

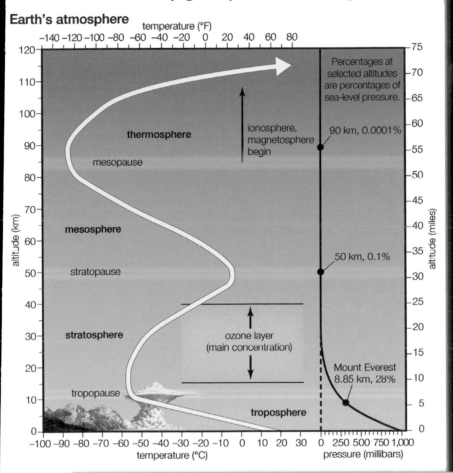

Earth's atmosphere

The temperature and pressure of the air vary with height. Temperatures, indicated by the yellow line, drop with altitude in some zones but rise in others. Pressures, indicated by the black line at right, decrease greatly with height. Encyclopædia Britannica, Inc.

the atmosphere, called the troposphere, temperature generally drops with increasing height. At a height of about 7 miles (11 kilometers), but somewhat higher over the tropics and lower over the poles, the temperature has reached approximately -70 °F (-57 °C). This point, the "top" of the troposphere, is called the tropopause. Almost all of Earth's "weather" (meaning precipitation, especially) occurs in the troposphere.

Above that, however, temperatures stay about the same and then actually begin to rise with height. This zone is called the stratosphere. Most of its surprising warmth—up to the freezing point of water or slightly higher—results from the interception of ultraviolet solar energy by ozone. Because of this temperature structure, the air in the stratosphere is very stable, meaning very little vertical mixing can occur. For this reason, volcanic dust or man-made gases that reach the stratosphere can remain stuck there for years. This also makes the stratosphere very dry, since very little water vapor is able to mix up into it from below.

The stratopause, the top of the stratosphere, is about 30 miles (50 kilometers) up. Above this is the mesosphere, a zone in which temperatures fall once again. After bottoming out at the mesopause, at roughly 50 miles (80 kilometers) up, temperatures become very high in the thermosphere, reaching over 2,000 °F (1,100 °C). This is misleading, however, because by this point the air is so thin that there is almost nothing there to feel. It simply means that the relatively few particles (mostly ions, or electrically charged atoms) present are moving quite fast. Beyond the thermosphere, one can define another region, the exosphere. This is an extremely rarified gas of mainly hydrogen and helium, which merges with the near vacuum of interplanetary space.

The atmosphere's pressure drops considerably with height, for a very simple reason. The pressure exerted by the air at any height is due to the weight of all the air above it. At great altitudes, there is little air above, so the pressure, and in turn density, becomes quite low. Pressure at sea level averages about 14.7 pounds per square inch (101,320 newtons per square meter), or one "atmosphere" (a unit of pressure). Roughly speaking, pressure is cut in half with every additional 3.5 miles (5.6 kilometers) above the ground. At an altitude of 7 miles, air pressure is about one fourth that at sea level.

AIR MOVEMENTS AND WEATHER

The atmosphere is constantly in motion, mainly because of pressure differences, which are in turn caused by differences in heating by the Sun. This solar energy is redistributed by winds, infrared radiation, and water vapor, resulting in the changing state of the atmosphere called the weather.

The circulation pattern of the atmosphere changes from day to day and from season to season. However, some definite overall patterns can be discerned. Air near the Equator is generally heated the most, which makes it less dense and causes the atmosphere in that region to expand upward. This often produces clouds and rain, making the tropics relatively wet. Air at high altitudes then flows poleward. Earth's rotation comes into play, though, via the Coriolis effect, which deflects the air to the right of the winds' direction of motion in the Northern Hemisphere and to the left in the Southern Hemisphere. This results in high altitude winds mainly from west to east in the middle latitudes.

Some of the poleward-flowing air sinks back toward the surface at about 25 or 30 degrees of latitude from the Equator in both hemispheres. This air then flows back toward

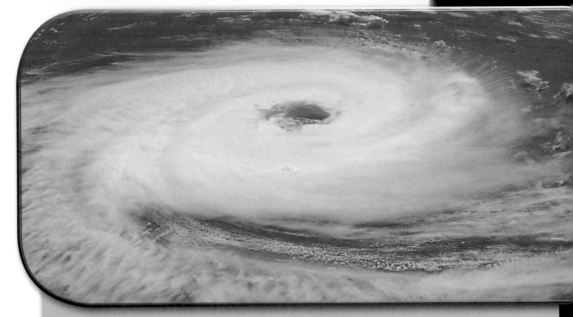

The tropical cyclone Catarina (2004)—the first documented storm to reach hurricane strength in the South Atlantic Basin—as seen from the International Space Station. Tropical cyclones have an impact on Earth's atmosphere. NASA

the Equator near the surface but is deflected by the Coriolis effect, becoming the trade winds. The trade winds blow from the northeast in the Northern Hemisphere and from the southeast in the Southern Hemisphere. Where the air is sinking, relatively high surface pressures are produced. The sinking air is compressed and warmed, so that clouds tend to evaporate and there is little rain. Most of the world's deserts are located in these subtropical regions.

Winds in the middle latitudes tend to be from the west on average. Closer to the poles winds tend to flow from the northeast in the Northern Hemisphere and the southeast in the Southern Hemisphere, much like the trade winds. A fairly distinct boundary between the relatively warm mid-latitude westerly (blowing from west to east) winds and the cold polar easterly winds can often be found. It is along this "polar front" that low-pressure systems called cyclones frequently form. An overall effect of these storms is to send colder air toward low latitudes and warmer air toward the poles.

In addition to mid-latitude cyclones, very strong tropical cyclones such as hurricanes and typhoons (two names for the same type of storm, applied to different regions) form in summer or fall. These storms eventually carry heat to high latitudes. In fact, the weather generally has the effect of making the Equator cooler than it would otherwise be and the poles warmer than they would be.

HYDROSPHERE

The hydrosphere includes all the liquid water on or just below the surface of the planet, the vast majority of which is in the oceans.

Some of Earth's water is frozen, mainly in Antarctica and Greenland. This ice and snow is called the cryosphere and is often included with the hydrosphere (as is done in this book). About 71 percent of Earth's surface is covered by oceans, with only a few percent covered by smaller bodies of water or by ice. The water vapor in the atmosphere can also be considered part of the hydrosphere (as is done here).

MASS AND COMPOSITION

The total mass of the hydrosphere is about 1.4 × 10^{21} kilograms (1.4 billion gigatons), which weighs about 3.1 × 10^{21} pounds. The mass of the hydrosphere is about 270 times the mass of the atmosphere. However, it is still less than $\frac{1}{4,000}$ of Earth's total mass. The oceans make up almost 98 percent of the hydrosphere's mass. By some estimates, ice caps and glaciers constitute almost 1.7 percent, with underground reservoirs accounting for about 0.37 percent. Freshwater in lakes and streams is only a tenth as abundant as groundwater, making up some 0.036 percent of the total. About 0.001 percent of Earth's water can be found in the atmosphere as water vapor or cloud droplets and ice crystals. If all the water vapor in the atmosphere

at a given time were condensed into liquid and spread over Earth's entire surface, it would form a layer about an inch (2.5 centimeters) thick.

The average depth of the oceans is about 12,400 feet, or 2.3 miles (3.8 kilometers). Even the deepest part, the Mariana Trench in the western North Pacific— 6.86 miles (11.03 kilometers) deep—extends only about $\frac{1}{600}$ of the way to Earth's center. So, like the atmosphere, the hydrosphere forms a relatively thin skin on the planet's surface.

A notable feature of the oceans is that they contain a great deal of dissolved salts, mainly sodium chloride (ordinary table salt). On average, there are about 3.5 kilograms of salt for every 100 kilograms of seawater. If the oceans were to completely evaporate, the remaining compacted salt would form deposits averaging at least 200 feet (60 meters) thick.

TEMPERATURE AND PRESSURE

Very little light penetrates more than about 100 feet (30 meters) into the water, so the depths of the ocean are pitch black. Temperatures become cold near the bottom, even in tropical seas, dropping as low as about 36 °F (2 °C). This is largely due to cold, dense salty water from the polar regions settling near the bottom of the world's oceans.

Since water is much denser than air, pressure changes in the vertical are much more dramatic in water than in air. Pressure in water increases by the equivalent of one atmosphere, or 14.7 pounds per square inch, for every 33 feet (10 meters) of depth. The ocean bottom has several hundred atmospheres of pressure, or several hundred times the pressure at sea level on land.

CURRENTS

Like the atmosphere, the oceans have large scale motions, or currents, which play an important role in redistributing the heat Earth receives from the Sun. Huge ocean currents, driven mainly by winds, circulate basically clockwise in the Northern Hemisphere and counterclockwise in the Southern Hemisphere. These currents bring cold water toward the Equator on the west coasts of continents and warm water toward the poles on east coasts.

In North America the cold California Current makes places such as San Francisco surprisingly cool, most notably in summer.

Diagram of currents in the world's oceans. **Dorling Kindersley/ Getty Images**

The warm Gulf Stream flowing north near the eastern coast of the continent keeps eastern beaches warmer and also strengthens hurricanes approaching the coast.

PRECIPITATION AND AQUIFERS

Evaporation of water from the oceans supplies almost all the moisture for precipitation.

Rain falling on the continents dissolves minerals, such as salt, which flow into and become concentrated in the oceans. On land much of the water flows visibly at the surface as rivers, but a great deal also goes underground, saturating deep layers of rock in reservoirs called aquifers. Many desert regions have aquifers deep underground holding water from rain that fell thousands of years ago. Wells that tap into these aquifers have been used for thousands of years.

LITHOSPHERE

"Lithos" means "rock," and the lithosphere consists of the outer, rocky parts of the planet. The name generally refers to Earth's crust and some of the upper mantle. The lithosphere has been found to make gradual movements, which sometimes bring fresh material to the surface and also bury older parts of the surface. Over vast amounts of time, much of the material is therefore recycled. During this process, it affects, and is affected by, the atmosphere, hydrosphere, and biosphere.

The lithosphere is broken into several "plates" that essentially float on the denser material underneath and drift up against, alongside, over, or underneath other plates.

Numerous kinds of green plants grow in profusion in a rainforest in Dominica. The existence of nearly the entire biosphere—including people and all other animals—depends on the photosynthesis carried out by the world's green plants and certain algae and bacteria. **Randolph Femmer/NBII Image Gallery**

This process is called plate tectonics. The movement of the plates relative to one another accounts for the formation of mountains and the occurrence of earthquakes and volcanoes.

BIOSPHERE

The biosphere is the "zone of life," consisting of all of Earth's living things and their environments. It is not really a separate sphere from the others but includes parts of all three. Life obviously occupies the oceans and the surfaces of the continents, but it also exists in the atmosphere. Birds and insects are obvious examples, but smaller organisms such as bacteria that become airborne can be carried miles above the surface. Additionally, bacteria have been found in rock 1.7 miles (2.8 kilometers) underground.

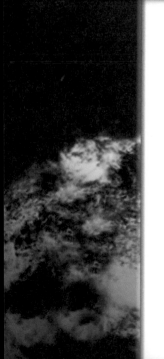

Life in Extreme Places

In recent decades, scientists have found ecosystems (groups of interdependent organisms and their environment) independent of sunlight. An example is the communities of creatures thriving around hydrothermal vents in the deep ocean. These vents spew hot water, laden with sulfur dioxide gas, from the ocean floor. Bacteria called chemoautotrophs make their food (sugars, as in photosynthesis) by using these hot gases along with carbon dioxide. Other creatures, such as long, red tube worms, store the bacteria in their bodies and live off their energy. Bacteria that have been found in deep underground rocks may be using hydrogen to make their food. The hydrogen may come from water broken apart by the nuclear radiation from radioactive elements, such as uranium, trapped in the rock.

Recently, many biologists have decided that some microorganisms inhabiting extreme environments (such as those with very hot or salty conditions) are not true bacteria. A new kingdom of such creatures, called Archaea, has been proposed, with the creatures called the archaeans. Finding organisms in such surprising environments has led some scientists to speculate that life could exist beneath the surface of Mars or in the deep, ice-covered oceans of Jupiter's moon Europa.

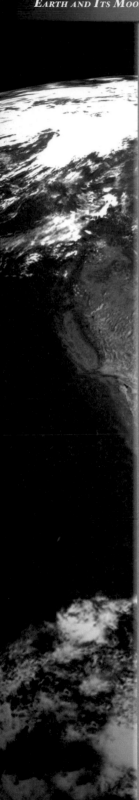

The biosphere plays a vital role in the chemistry and geologic processes of the planet. Earth, especially the outer layers, is a very different world than it would be with no life. The biosphere is thought to have almost completely buried an ancient atmosphere of mainly carbon dioxide, replacing some of it with oxygen. It has also produced vast deposits of coal and oil and has even regulated the planet's temperature.

Most of the biosphere is based on the process of photosynthesis, by which plants and some microorganisms use sunlight to convert water, carbon dioxide (from the atmosphere), and minerals into oxygen (which then enters the atmosphere) and simple and complex sugars. Animals eat many of these plants and microorganisms, thus consuming much of their stored energy. Energy is concentrated further into a small number of carnivores, who eat other animals. Scavengers eat dead plants and animals. After all of the above creatures die, they are gradually buried in the ground or sink to the seafloor. In this way, they are eventually incorporated into Earth's lithosphere, with some gases, such as methane, being released into the atmosphere or hydrosphere.

EARTH'S CYCLES

M any of Earth's materials are recycled in various ways through Earth's spheres. Life plays an essential role in many of these cycles, in effect regulating the environment, often in a way that is beneficial for life. Two of the most important cycles are the water cycle and the carbon cycle.

WATER CYCLE

The water, or hydrologic, cycle can be thought to begin—though cycles do not necessarily have a "beginning"—when the Sun's heat evaporates water from the oceans. This water enters the atmosphere as vapor. About 100,000 cubic miles (over 400,000 cubic kilometers) of seawater evaporate each year. If this water were not returned to the oceans and the water continued to evaporate at the same rate, the sea level would drop by almost 4 feet (about 1.2 meters) per year and the oceans would be gone within 3,500 years.

Of course, this water is eventually returned. Precipitation falling directly on the oceans amounts to just over 90 percent of the water

Earth's water cycle. **Encyclopædia Britannica, Inc.**

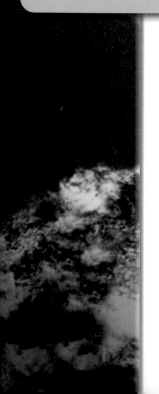

evaporated from them. The remainder flows back into the ocean from land, carried mainly in rivers. Precipitation also falls on land—about the same amount per square mile as the ocean receives—totaling about 26,000 cubic miles (107,000 cubic kilometers). Plants draw water from the soil and, in a process called transpiration, release water vapor into the air through tiny pores in their leaves. About 17,000 cubic miles (70,000 cubic kilometers) of water enters the atmosphere over land in this way and from evaporation off the land. This leaves about 9,000 cubic miles (37,000 cubic kilometers) traveling from land to water via rivers each year.

THE WATER TABLE

Much of the water that falls on land does not immediately enter streams and rivers. Instead, it filters through porous soil and rock into the ground. At varying depths under the surface, it often saturates the porous rock, forming the "water table." Such water may remain underground for hundreds of years, but most of it eventually finds its way into streams and enters the oceans after all.

How the Water Table Looks in a Cross Section of Land

unsaturated soil

water table

surface water

ground water

The water table is the top level of groundwater. Surface water is an exposed part of the water table. Copyright Encyclopædia Britannica, Inc.; rendering for this edition by Rosen Educational Services

PLATE TECTONICS AND THE WATER CYCLE

One part of the water cycle is sometimes overlooked. This is the chemical combining of ocean water with rocks on the seafloor and its eventual release in volcanic gases. Such "hydrated" rocks have a lower melting point than they would otherwise. As the various plates of the lithosphere move, the seafloor on one plate is sometimes pushed against the edge of a continent on another. The denser oceanic crust is forced under the continental crust, and the "hydrated" rocks of the seafloor melt readily. This has a lubricating effect on plate motion, so that the water cycle is actually tied in with plate tectonics. Plumes of molten material and gases, including water vapor that was once part of the sea, rise to the surface in volcanoes. This water then enters the atmosphere after a residence time of tens, or even hundreds, of millions of years in the oceanic crust.

RESIDENCE TIME

As a material—in this case water—moves among various reservoirs, any given molecule will spend a characteristic time, called the residence time, in each reservoir. Typically, a water molecule will remain in the atmosphere a bit over a week before falling to the ground as precipitation (or possibly forming dew or frost). Shallow soil moisture or seasonal snow cover may last months. Glaciers and lakes hold water for decades. Residence time in the ocean is a few thousand years.

CARBON CYCLE

Carbon makes up only about 0.03 percent of Earth's crust by weight. Its principal form in the atmosphere—carbon dioxide—makes up only about 0.04 percent of the atmosphere. However, this element is the basis of all known life and also plays a vital role in maintaining habitable conditions on Earth. How it is cycled through the environment is therefore of great interest. The carbon cycle is the complex path that carbon follows through the atmosphere, oceans, and soil; through plants and animals; and through fossil fuel formation and use.

CARBON STORAGE

The vast majority—over 99.9 percent—of Earth's near-surface carbon (carbon in the lithosphere and above) is stored in sedimentary rock. Estimates vary, but this reservoir probably holds roughly 80 million gigatons

CARBON CYCLE

free CO₂ gas

assimilation into soil

combustion

marine deposits of CaCO₃

assimilation by plants and animals

animal respiration

plant respiration

fossil fuel formation

peat
coal
oil

organic decomposition

use of fossil fuels

of carbon. This carbon was deposited over billions of years, partly by the weathering of silicate rocks to form carbonate rocks, which contain carbon compounds. It also accumulated from the remains of marine organisms that had used carbon to build calcium carbonate shells or body parts.

The next most abundant storage site is the deep ocean, which holds about 38,000 gigatons of carbon. Fossil fuels—coal, oil, and natural gas—make up an estimated 5,000 gigatons. The rest of the carbon is divided roughly equally among living plants (about 600

Earth's carbon cycle. **Encyclopædia Britannica, Inc.**

gigatons), organic debris in soil (about 1,600 gigatons), the near-surface ocean (about 1,000 gigatons), and the atmosphere (nearly 800 gigatons and increasing).

The deep ocean and the near-surface ocean are listed separately because the two do not mix very quickly. Thousands of years may be needed for changes near the surface to work their way down to the bottom. The

Mussels collected on rocks at South Africa's Pinnacle Point. The calcium carbonate in the shells of mussels and other mollusks contributes to Earth's carbon stores. **Per-Anders Pettersson/Getty Images**

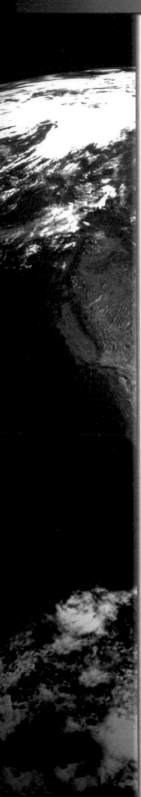

oceans in general have a great capacity to store carbon. However, the short-term (such as decades) storage is mainly in the upper layers, which have limited capacity.

RESIDENCE TIME

The carbon cycle is quite complex, partly because life plays many roles in it, but also because of the huge range of residence times involved. The largest reservoir, sedimentary rock, also has the longest residence time. Carbon has been steadily buried in rock throughout Earth's history and is released a little at a time, primarily through volcanic activity. A carbon atom might spend hundreds of millions of years locked away in rock before being released in the gases of a volcano. Probably most carbon atoms ever trapped in rock have never been released and may never be. Nevertheless, this geologic carbon cycle is of great importance. Over long periods the burial and release of carbon dioxide (and also methane) largely control Earth's surface temperature. Higher amounts of these gases in the distant past likely helped warm the planet when the Sun was less bright in its youth.

Carbon travels rather quickly— generally a matter of months, years, or

CARBON AND HUMAN ACTIVITY

Fossil fuels are a complicated part of the carbon cycle because they took millions of years to be formed and buried but are being released by humans rather quickly. From the beginning of the Industrial Revolution in the mid-18th century to the start of the 21st century, roughly 300 gigatons of carbon were released by humans burning these fuels — over half of that after 1970. In the early 21st century such use was releasing over 6 gigatons of carbon per year, a rate thousands of times that at which it was originally buried.

While human-induced release of carbon accounts for only a few percentage of the total entering the atmosphere, it is important to understand that this disrupts an otherwise fairly delicate balance. Much, perhaps half, of it ends up as excess carbon dioxide in the atmosphere, where it contributes to global warming. Besides burning fossil fuels, humans alter the balance in other ways. Deforestation, some farming practices, and the manufacture of cement also contribute to increasing the carbon content of the atmosphere.

decades—among the remaining reservoirs. Plants take about 120 gigatons of carbon per year from the atmosphere during photosynthesis, which releases oxygen. However, they return about half of that carbon by respiration, which uses oxygen, largely at night. Also, some of the carbon in plants is eaten by herbivores and released during the herbivores' respiration, or during the respiration of carnivores that eat the herbivores. Much of the dead plant and animal matter in the soil is consumed by bacteria and fungi, which release carbon dioxide (or methane, if deprived of oxygen).

Just over 90 gigatons of carbon enter the ocean each year, largely by being dissolved from the air. Plankton in the ocean perform photosynthesis on a scale similar to that of land plants. Some of the carbon that enters the ocean is buried in ocean sediments, but much is released, some through the respiration of creatures that eat the plankton. All but perhaps two gigatons is released back into the atmosphere per year.

Earth's Satellite: The Moon

The most prominent feature in the night sky is Earth's natural satellite, the Moon. Because of its nearness to Earth, the Moon is second only to the Sun in apparent brightness among celestial objects. It also appears roughly the same size as the Sun, though the Sun is actually about 400 times larger and 400 times more distant.

The Moon's prominence in the sky and its regular cycles have captured the interest of people worldwide through all of recorded history. It has been the subject of legends, superstitions, and sayings. The Moon has been suspected of causing or curing diseases, aiding or retarding the growth of crops, altering the weather, and bringing either good or bad luck to those who see it. One such belief was that sleeping under moonlight would render one "moonstruck," or mad. Such a person would then be a "lunatic" (from the Latin word *luna*, meaning "Moon").

On a scientific level, the Moon has been an object of investigation for centuries. Early studies of the Moon allowed the prediction of tides and led to the development of calendars.

The familiar near side of the Moon appears in an image taken in 1992 by the Galileo spacecraft while on its way to Jupiter. The lighter areas are heavily cratered ancient highlands, while the darker areas are younger lava-filled impact basins. **Photo NASA/JPL/Caltech (NASA photo # PIA00405)**

The Moon was the first new world on which humans set foot, and lunar missions have led to a knowledge of the Moon that surpasses that of any other cosmic body except Earth itself.

Earth and the Moon exert a strong gravitational pull on each other, forming a system with complex properties and motions. Although it is commonly said that the Moon orbits Earth, the two bodies actually orbit each other about a common center of mass, called the barycenter. The barycenter lies within the outer portion of Earth's interior. As the Earth-Moon system orbits the Sun, both bodies also rotate on their axes. Earth's axis is tilted about 23.5° from the ecliptic plane, which is the imaginary plane in which its orbit lies.

Geometry and motions of the Earth-Moon system

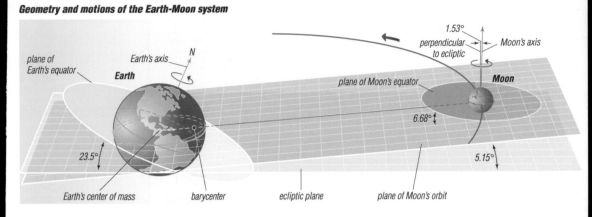

The gravitational give-and-take between Earth and the Moon. Encyclopædia Britannica, Inc.

THE MOON'S APPEARANCE FROM EARTH

The Moon is most obvious at night, though it is commonly visible in the daytime as well. Like most celestial bodies, it is above the horizon about half the time. The sunlit side of the Moon appears quite brilliant in the dark night sky. If compared to other objects in the sunlight, however, it is actually a somewhat dark gray, reflecting only about 7 percent of the visible sunlight that hits it. To the naked eye, only a few features are visible on its surface, most notably the smooth, dark maria—or plains—which form a pattern

The full Moon rises over Grand Canyon National Park in Arizona.
Robert Glusic/Getty Images

sometimes referred to as "the man in the Moon." A sharp eye may reveal the bright streaks radiating from a couple of the larger craters, such as one called Tycho.

Observation of these features readily reveals an interesting fact: the Moon always keeps the same side (the "near side") toward Earth, while nearly half of its surface (the "far side") can never be seen from here. This occurs because the Moon revolves around Earth at

THE MOON ILLUSION

Most people think the Moon looks much larger when near the horizon than when high in the sky. This is a perceptual effect, commonly known as the "Moon illusion." Explanations of the illusion's causes generally depend on the presence of distance cues near the horizon or the lack of such cues when the Moon is high in the sky. Just how such cues lead to the illusion is a matter of contention, however. Aside from this illusion, though, there are small changes in the apparent size of the Moon because it is not always equally far from Earth in its orbit. Its apogee (greatest distance from Earth) is up to 13 percent greater than its perigee (closest point to Earth).

the same average rate at which it rotates on its axis. Over time, however, the slight noncircularity of the Moon's orbit, combined with its steady rotation, docs render about 59 percent of the surface visible from Earth. There is not a permanent "dark side" or "bright side" of the Moon; the near and far sides get equal amounts of sunlight over time.

Sometimes the Moon appears yellowish, orange, or almost red. This generally happens when the Moon is close to the horizon, and its light must traverse a long path through

Earth's atmosphere before reaching the observer. The shorter, bluer wavelengths of light are largely scattered away, leaving mainly reddish colors. This effect is not unique to the Moon. The Sun also looks more reddish near sunset and sunrise.

THE MOON THROUGH A TELESCOPE

The Italian scientist Galileo Galilei was the first person known to have used a telescope for astronomy, turning one of his own making to the study of the Moon in 1609. He immediately saw that it was not the perfectly smooth sphere proposed by Aristotle and most astronomers after him. There were cup-shaped valleys (craters) and mountains, in addition to the smooth areas visible to the naked eye. Galileo noted that in these ways the Moon seemed rather similar to Earth, suggesting that the two bodies were of a similar nature. In fact, Galileo considered this an important piece of evidence supporting the Copernican theory that Earth is a body orbiting the Sun; if the Moon moves and is similar to Earth, then maybe Earth moves, too.

Today, even small telescopes used by amateur astronomers show much more detail

The crater-pocked surface of the far side of the Moon was photographed by astronauts of the Apollo 11 mission in July 1969. **NASA**

than did Galileo's instrument. Thousands of craters of varying sizes are visible, some overlapping or embedded within others and many showing "rays" of lighter-colored material radiating from them. Mountain ranges rim the maria, which themselves have relatively few craters. Long valleys called rilles are visible in places. Most of these features are most dramatic when they are located near the terminator—the dividing

line between lunar day and night—because they then cast long, sharp shadows.

PHASES OF THE MOON

The angle between the Sun and the Moon in the sky determines what fraction of the side of the Moon facing Earth is lit, giving rise to the succession of phases. The phase cycle is often considered to start with the "new" Moon, which is invisible from Earth. In this phase the Moon is almost or directly between Earth and the Sun, so the entire sunlit portion of the Moon faces away from Earth. The Moon's orbit carries it eastward relative to the Sun in the sky, so that a few days after new, the Moon appears in the early evening as a crescent, with the lit side facing west, toward where the Sun has just set. The rest of the Moon's disk may be faintly visible from light reflected off Earth. This crescent Moon sets a few hours after the Sun.

About a week after new, the Moon appears half lit and high in the sky, 90 degrees east of the Sun, at sunset. This Moon, called first quarter (being a quarter of the way through its monthly cycle), will have risen at about noon and may have been visible in a blue sky during the afternoon. For the next few nights, the Moon comes up later in the afternoon and continues

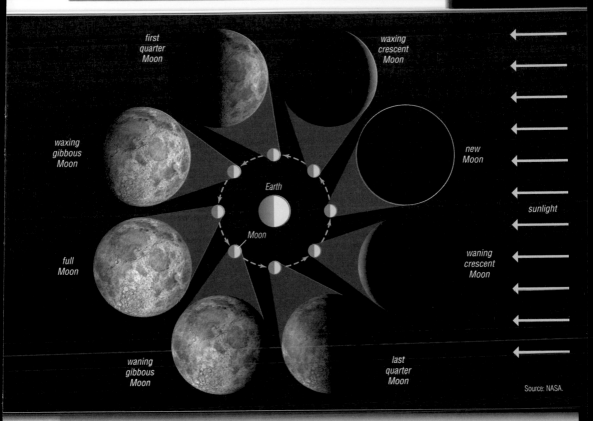

first quarter Moon

waxing crescent Moon

waxing gibbous Moon

Earth

new Moon

Moon

sunlight

full Moon

waning crescent Moon

waning gibbous Moon

last quarter Moon

Source: NASA.

The Sun always illuminates half of the Moon, but varying amounts of the sunlit part are visible from Earth as the Moon orbits Earth and the two bodies circle the Sun. A diagram shows the position of the Moon in each of its phases, relative to Earth and the Sun and as seen from above Earth's North Pole. The photographs show how the Moon appears to observers in the Northern Hemisphere on Earth in each phase. **Encyclopædia Britannica, Inc. Photos Yerkes Observatory, University of Chicago**

to wax, or show a greater illuminated fraction. During this time it is referred to as gibbous, or between half and full. About two weeks after new, it rises as a full Moon more or less in the

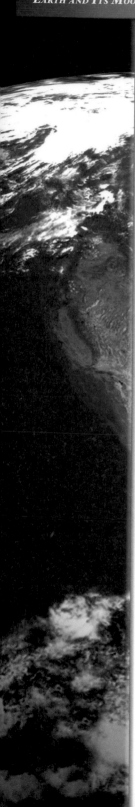

east—opposite the Sun—at sunset. The full Moon stays up all night, setting more or less in the west at about sunrise.

After its full phase, the Moon rises later and later each evening, passing through waning (progressively less illuminated) gibbous phases. Then, at third quarter, it appears as a "half" Moon with its eastern half lit. In this phase, the Moon rises at about midnight, is highest at sunrise, and sets at about noon. Finally, after a few days of waning crescents, the Moon returns to new, 29.53 days after the last new Moon. Actually, the Moon orbits Earth with a period of 27.32 days, but during this time Earth will have moved almost $\frac{1}{12}$ of the way around the Sun, so 2.21 extra days are needed for the Moon to get back to its position between Earth and the Sun.

ECLIPSES

The Moon's path through the sky, as seen against the background of stars, is very close to the Sun's path, called the ecliptic. For this reason, it is possible at new Moon for the Moon to pass directly between Earth and the Sun, casting its shadow on Earth. During such an event—called a solar eclipse—the Moon partially or totally blocks the Sun's light. If the Moon is a bit closer to Earth than on average, it appears large enough in the sky to completely cover the Sun's disk for up to about 7 minutes. Such total eclipses are spectacular events, with the Sun's corona, or outer atmosphere, visible around the black disk of the Moon in a daytime sky nearly as dark as night. The path of total eclipse is typically only about 100 miles (160 kilometers) wide. Observers in the area around the path of totality see only part of the Sun blocked, and people outside that area do not see an eclipse.

It is also possible for Earth to be exactly between the Sun and the Moon, thereby casting a shadow on the Moon. This is called a lunar eclipse, and it naturally happens at full Moon. If the Moon passes completely into Earth's shadow, the eclipse is called total and the previously full Moon almost completely disappears from the night sky. Only dim reddish sunlight refracted onto the Moon by Earth's atmosphere renders it visible.

If the Moon's and Sun's apparent paths in the sky were identical, lunar and solar eclipses would happen every month. However, the Moon's orbit is inclined about 5 degrees relative to Earth's orbit around the Sun, so that the alignment is usually not good enough for either type of eclipse to occur.

PHYSICAL CHARACTERISTICS OF THE MOON

I n astronomical terms, the Moon is a fairly ordinary rocky object. Its light is simply reflected sunlight, with dim reflected light from Earth sometimes visible on the part not lit by the Sun. It orbits Earth just as many dozens of other satellites, or moons, orbit other planets in the solar system. In fact, five of those moons are actually larger than "our" Moon.

The Moon is rather large in comparison to its primary planet, though, being over a quarter the diameter of Earth. Only the dwarf planet Pluto's satellite Charon has a larger relative size—over half the diameter of Pluto itself. The Moon's relatively large size gives it a significant influence on Earth, most evident in the ocean tides, which are a result of the Moon's gravitational pull on Earth and its oceans.

SIZE AND DISTANCE FROM EARTH

The approximate distance and size of the Moon have been known for over 1,800 years. In the 3rd century BC, Aristarchus of Samos noted the apparent size of Earth's shadow as the Moon passed through it during lunar eclipses.

This observation enabled him to calculate very roughly the Moon's size and distance relative to Earth's diameter. In the 2nd century BC, the Greek astronomer Hipparchus improved these estimates. He noted that when a solar eclipse had been seen to be total in the Hellespont region of what is now western Turkey, only four fifths of the Sun's disk had been covered as seen from Alexandria, Egypt. Using early trigonometry and knowing the approximate distance between these two places, he was able to calculate the Moon's distance as roughly 63 times Earth's radius. In around AD 150, Ptolemy of Alexandria refined this value to about 60 Earth radii, or 30 Earth diameters—essentially the modern known value. He was able to determine from this and the Moon's apparent angular size of about half a degree that the Moon's diameter is just over one quarter of Earth's.

The modern value for the Moon's average distance from Earth's center is 238,900 miles (384,400 kilometers). It ranges, however, from about 225,700 miles (363,300 kilometers) at mean perigee to some 252,000 miles (405,500 kilometers) at mean apogee. The Moon's diameter is 2,157 miles (3,472 kilometers) from pole to pole and 2,160 miles (3,476 kilometers) at the Equator, or about 27 percent the diameter of Earth.

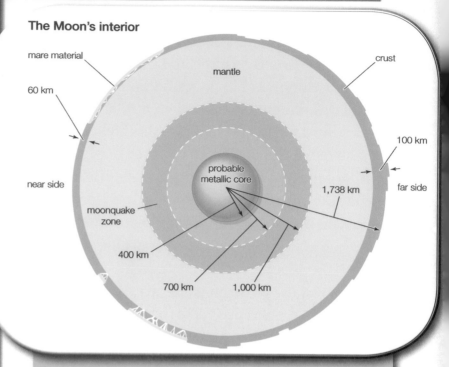

The Moon's interior

mare material

60 km

near side

moonquake zone

400 km

700 km

1,000 km

mantle

probable metallic core

1,738 km

crust

100 km

far side

A drawing shows a cross section of the Moon. The indicated distances are not to scale. Encyclopædia Britannica, Inc.

MASS AND DENSITY

Attempts to determine the Moon's mass considered its gravitational effects. Various efforts, including those of Pierre-Simon Laplace (1749–1827), used studies of ocean tides to refine this value, which turns out to be 7.35×10^{22} kilograms, or about $\frac{1}{81}$ that of Earth. The value is now particularly well known from data from numerous spacecraft

THE MOON AND OCEAN TIDES

The Moon and Earth, like all other pairs of masses in the universe, gravitationally attract one another. The strength of this force decreases with distance, so that the Moon pulls harder on the side of Earth nearest it than it does on the far side. This difference in force causes a slight stretching of Earth, most obvious in the fluid body of the oceans, along the direction of the line from Earth to the Moon. Isaac Newton correctly identified this as the cause of the tides. Generally, high tide occurs on both the side of Earth facing the Moon and the side away from it, with low tide in areas with the Moon close to the horizon.

This picture is complicated by many factors. The Sun produces almost half as much stretching as does the Moon, and Earth's rotation effectively carries the tidal bulge ahead of where it would otherwise be. When the Sun, Earth, and Moon are aligned at new or full Moon, the tides are more pronounced than usual, a situation called "spring tide." When they are at right angles (at first or third quarter Moon), the tides are reduced in amplitude and called "neap tides."

that have orbited the Moon. The acceleration due to gravity on the Moon is 5.32 feet (1.62 meters) per second per second, or about one sixth that on Earth. Someone weighing

100 pounds on Earth would weigh only about 16.5 pounds on the Moon.

The Moon's mean density is 3.34 grams per cubic centimeter, or about 60 percent of Earth's. This is important because it shows that the Moon must be composed, on average, of materials somewhat less dense than those that make up Earth. In particular, while the outer layers of the Moon are thought to be roughly similar to the outer layers of Earth, the Moon is thought to have an iron-rich core that is proportionally far smaller than Earth's. Probably related to this is the fact that the Moon has almost no coordinated magnetic field. Only weak, locally varying magnetic fields are present, and they were probably frozen into the crust at formation.

COMPOSITION AND ATMOSPHERE

The Moon's surface consists of rocky material, much of it pulverized into dust and other small fragments by billions of years of bombardment by meteorites, large and small. This layer, called regolith, varies in thickness from about 10 to 50 feet (3 to 15 meters). Underneath this is a rocky crust, ranging in thickness from very thin in some areas to over 60 miles (about 100 kilometers) in parts of the Moon's far side. Much of the rest of the Moon is a mantle of semi-molten rock, believed to surround a small, metallic core.

The Moon has almost no atmosphere, which accounts for the black sky in spite of bright sunshine seen in pictures taken from the surface by astronauts of the Apollo missions. Very small amounts of gases such as helium, hydrogen, argon, and neon have been detected, but with a surface density of only about a quadrillionth that of Earth's atmosphere. This lack of air, combined with days over two weeks long followed by equally long nights, allows the surface to reach extremely high and low temperatures. On average, surface temperatures reach about 225 °F (107 °C) in the day but

The cohesiveness of the lunar soil can be seen in a crisply defined boot print left on the Moon by U.S. astronaut Edwin Aldrin during the Apollo 11 mission in July 1969. Aldrin photographed the print as part of a study of the nature of the soil and its compaction behavior. The image has also become an icon of the first visit by humans to another world. **NASA**

then fall to about - 243 °F (- 153 °C) at night. In some areas, however, the temperature may be as high as about 253 °F (123 °C) or as low as about - 387 °F (- 233 °C).

LUNAR GEOGRAPHY

Relatively light-colored and heavily cratered highlands cover about 83 percent of the Moon's surface, while most of the remainder consists of smoother, darker patches—the maria. These features are not evenly distributed, however; nearly all the maria are on the near side. The maria are actually misnamed. Early telescopic observers thought that the dark smooth areas they saw might be bodies of water, so they called them "maria," meaning "seas" in Latin (with "mare" being the singular form). It is now known that the Moon has no seas, lakes, rivers, or liquid water of any kind. The maria are dry plains.

ROCKS AND CRATERS

The Apollo missions returned rocks from both types of terrain. Radioactive dating of these samples shows that the rocks taken from the maria range from about 3.1 billion to 3.9 billion years old, while those from the highlands are mostly between 4.0 billion and 4.5 billion years old. The maria rocks are largely basalt, a volcanic rock common on Earth, while the highlands consist largely of anorthosite, another type of igneous rock.

Craters are circular depressions on the surface of the Moon. They range in size from the tiny pits seen by Apollo astronauts, to numerous depressions more than 100 miles (160 kilometers) across and a couple of miles deep, to the gigantic South Pole–Aitken Basin on the southern far side. This depression is over 1,500 miles (2,400 kilometers) in diameter and up to 8 miles (13 kilometers) deep in places. Many craters, such as the large craters Tycho and Copernicus, have light-colored rays projecting outward hundreds of miles in all directions.

Apollo 15 astronaut James B. Irwin loads equipment onto the back of the Lunar Roving Vehicle, right, on the surface of the Moon at the Hadley-Apennine landing site in July 1971. Samples from this and other Apollo missions gave scientists a clearer picture of the composition of the Moon's surface. **NASA**

LUNAR EXPLORATION

The Moon was an early target for missions for the United States and the Soviet Union during the "space race," which lasted from the late 1950s to the 1970s. The Soviets scored first, sending the unmanned Luna 1 past the Moon in January 1959. The United States followed with Pioneer 4 two months later. In September 1959 the Soviet Luna 2 became the first craft to strike the Moon's surface (as it was designed to do), and the next month Luna 3 radioed back the first photograph ever of the Moon's far side.

Both countries launched numerous unmanned lunar missions over the next few years. On Feb. 3, 1966, the Soviet craft Luna 9 successfully soft-landed and televised the first pictures from the surface of another world. The U.S. Surveyor 1 soft-landed and sent back pictures and other scientific data in June of that year.

The U.S. Apollo 8 was the first manned mission to the Moon. It carried three astronauts into lunar orbit

Luna 9 was the first spacecraft to soft-land on the Moon. It was launched by the Soviet Union on Jan. 31, 1966, and returned photographs of the lunar surface for three days. **Novosti Press Agency**

and back to Earth in December 1968. On July 20, 1969, Apollo 11's lunar module successfully landed on Mare Tranquillitatis (the "Sea" of Tranquillity), and Neil Armstrong and Buzz Aldrin became the first humans to set foot on the Moon. Five more successful Apollo landings (Apollo 13 was unable to land) followed.

Since the 1970s there have been no manned missions to the Moon, and no unmanned missions were sent until Japan's orbiter Hiten was launched in 1990. Later in the 1990s the United States launched the Clementine and Lunar Prospector orbiters, which mapped the entire Moon. In the early 21st century the United States continued to have the most ambitious exploration program, but an Asian space race led to a flurry of activity there. In 2007–08 Japan, China, and India all launched probes to the Moon; the Chinese and Indian missions were the first for those countries. In 2009 the Indian spacecraft Chandrayaan-1 found water molecules on the Moon.

THE EFFECTS OF BOMBARDMENTS

For many years scientists debated whether the craters arc primarily volcanic in origin or were caused by impacts of asteroids and comets. The latter explanation is now believed to account for the vast majority of craters. The form of the craters (including the rays of ejecta, or ejected debris) is what would be expected from impacts, and current theories of the solar system's formation

feature a period of heavy bombardment early in the solar system's history. Some craters are present on Earth, too. In fact, most astronomers believe that the Moon itself formed from fragments created when a larger object slammed into Earth. Most of Earth's craters have been heavily eroded or subducted under other continental plates. The Moon preserves a much more pristine record of this early bombardment.

The generally accepted explanation for these observations is that after the Moon formed about 4.5 billion years ago, it was subject to frequent impacts as it swept up some of the debris of the early solar system. By about 4 billion years ago, the Moon would have looked much as it does today, except without the maria. Starting about 3.9 billion years ago, a series of major melting episodes, perhaps caused or aided by large impacts, melted large areas, mainly on the near side. The low areas filled with magma, which smoothed over the existing craters. Since most of the solar system's debris had been swept up by then, only a small number of impacts have occurred since—hence the smooth appearance of the maria, which are lower in elevation than the heavily cratered areas. An excellent example is the huge Mare Imbrium, some 800 miles

(1,300 kilometers) across and almost certainly caused by a giant impact.

A dramatic intensification of the impact rate, called the late heavy bombardment, is thought to have occurred on the Moon and elsewhere in the solar system roughly 3.9 billion years ago. The period of intense bombardment perhaps resulted from the late formation or migration outward of Uranus and Neptune, with icy bodies thereby being thrown from the outer solar system inward toward the Sun.

Mountains

Lunar mountains, some of which rival the Himalayas in height, are generally formed by rather different processes than on Earth. Most terrestrial mountains are a result of giant continental plates of Earth's crust having collided with or ridden up over others. Most lunar mountains are basically the rims of giant impact basins or, in some cases, central peaks of craters resulting from a sort of rebound effect after the impacts that formed the craters.

Ancient craters mark the surface of the far side of the Moon, shown in an image taken by the Apollo 16 spacecraft. **F.J. Doyle/ National Space Science Data Center**

CONCLUSION

For centuries people believed that Earth was the center of the universe. It was not until the 16th century that Copernicus correctly proposed that Earth revolves around the Sun. This revolutionary theory meant that Earth was not as exceptional as once had been thought. The stature of Earth was further diminished by later discoveries that the stars are also suns and that many have planets of their own. These facts can make Earth seem insignificant in the vastness of space. Yet it is highly significant to the organisms that call the planet home, including humans. Earth has many special properties and processes that are unique among the planets discovered so far.

The Moon is understood better by humankind than any body in space other than Earth. This satellite has rich potential as a source of materials and energy, and it is uniquely qualified as a laboratory for planetary science. Although many questions remain about its composition, structure, and history, the Moon no doubt holds keys to understanding the origin of Earth and the solar system.

apogee The point in the orbit of an object (as a satellite) orbiting Earth that is at the greatest distance from the center of Earth.

Coriolis effect The apparent acceleration of a moving body on or near Earth as a result of Earth's rotation; an important determinant of wind direction on a global scale.

crater A bowl-shaped depression or hole caused by the bombardment of asteroids, meteorites, or comets.

ecliptic The great circle that is the apparent path of the Sun; also, the plane of Earth's orbit.

equinox Either of the two times each year when the Sun crosses the Equator and day and night are of equal length.

geodesy A branch of applied mathematics concerned with the determination of Earth's size and shape.

lithosphere Rigid, rocky outer layer of Earth, consisting of the crust and the solid outermost layer of the upper mantle.

magma Molten rock beneath Earth's core; outside of Earth's surface from which igneous rocks form; molten rock on the surface called lava.

perigee The point in the orbit of an object (as a satellite) orbiting Earth that is nearest to the center of Earth.

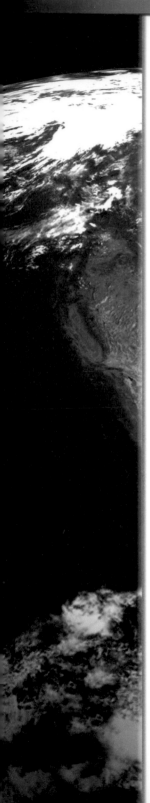

photosynthesis The process by which green plants and certain other organisms transform light energy into chemical energy.

pumice A volcanic glass full of cavities and very low in density that is used especially in powder form for smoothing and polishing.

regolith Unconsolidated residual or transported material that overlies the solid rock on Earth, the Moon, or another planet.

rille Any of several long, narrow valleys on the Moon's surface.

sedimentary Formed of or by material deposited by water, wind, or glaciers.

seismic Of or relating to an earth vibration caused by an earthquake or some other force (as an explosion or the impact of a meteorite).

sidereal Of, relating to, or expressed in relation to stars or constellations; astral.

terminator The dividing line between the illuminated and the unilluminated part of the Moon's or a planet's disk, marking day and night as observed from a distance.

tomography A method of producing a three-dimensional image of the internal structures of a solid object (as Earth) by observing and recording the differences in the effects on the passage of waves of energy impinging on a structure.

Canadian Space Agency
John H. Chapman Space Centre
6767 Route de l'Aéroport
Saint-Hubert, QB J3Y 8Y9
Canada
(450) 926-4800
Web site: http://www.asc-csa.gc.ca
The Canadian Space Agency offers information on Canada's space program, missions, and more. The site provides information on science fairs and camps, and podcasts on a variety of topics related to space exploration are available for download.

H.R. MacMillan Space Centre
1100 Chestnut Street.
Vancouver, BC V6J 3J9
Canada
(604) 738-7827
Web site: http://www.spacecentre.ca
The H.R. MacMillian Centre is a nonprofit community resource based in Vancouver, Canada. The center inspires interest in the universe, Earth, and space exploration through innovative programming, exhibits, and activities.

Lunar and Planetary Institute
3600 Bay Area Boulevard

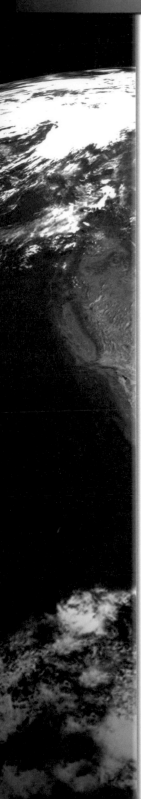

Houston, TX 77058
(281) 486-2100
Web site: http://www.lpi.usra.edu
The Lunar and Planetary Institute advances
    research in lunar and planetary science and
    offers a number of education and public out-
    reach programs as well as information on
    scholarships, contests, and more for students.

National Aeronautics and Space
    Administration
300 E Street SW
Washington, DC 20024
(202) 358-0001
Web site: http://www.nasa.gov
NASA offers information on the U.S. space
    program as well as innovative research in
    the field of aeronautics. The site includes
    games, activities, and other resources for
    students.

The Planetary Society
85 South Grand
Pasadena, CA 91105
(626) 793-5100
Web site: http://www.planetary.org
The Planetary Society is dedicated to
    increasing public interest in space and
    space exploration. Information on its

advocacy and education initiatives as well as its various projects is available online.

The Smithsonian Center for Earth and
    Planetary Studies
PO Box 37012
National Air and Space Museum, MRC 315
Washington, DC 20013-7012
(202) 633-2470
Web site: http://www.nasm.si.edu/ceps
The Center for Earth and Planetary Studies
    is a research unit of the Smithsonian's
    National Air and Space Museum. It
    uses data from Earth-orbiting satellites
    and from manned and unmanned space
    missions to examine the geological and
    geophysical attributes of Earth.

WEB SITES

Due to the changing nature of Internet links, Rosen Educational Services has developed an online list of Web sites related to the subject of this book. This site is updated regularly. Please use this link to access the list:

http://www.rosenlinks.com/tss/eart

Coenraads, R.R. *Rocks and Fossils* (Firefly, 2005).

Cullen, K.E. *Earth Science: The People Behind the Science* (Facts On File, 2006).

Fothergill, Alastair. *Planet Earth as You've Never Seen It Before* (Univ. Calif. Press, 2006).

Johnson, R.L. *Plate Tectonics* (Lerner, 2006).

Juniper, Tony. *Saving Planet Earth* (Collins, 2007).

Kerr Casper, Julie. *Water and Atmosphere: The Lifeblood of Natural Systems* (Chelsea, 2007).

Marshak, Stephen. *Earth*, 2nd ed. (Norton, 2005).

Miller, Ron. *Earth and the Moon: Worlds Beyond* (Twenty-First Century Books, 2003).

Pollock, Steve. *Ecology*, rev. ed. (DK, 2005).

Stille, D.R. *Erosion: How Land Forms, How It Changes* (Compass Point, 2005).

Stille, D.R. *Plate Tectonics: Earth's Moving Crust* (Compass Point, 2007).

Stow, D.A.V. *Oceans* (Univ. of Chicago Press, 2006).

Sussman, Art. *Dr. Art's Guide to Planet Earth: For Earthlings Ages 12 to 120* (Chelsea Green, 2000).

Thompson, D.M. *Processes That Shape the Earth* (Chelsea, 2007).

Vernon, R.H. *Beneath Our Feet: The Rocks of Planet Earth* (Cambridge Univ. Press, 2000).

Vogt, G.L. *The Atmosphere; The Biosphere; Earth's Core and Mantle; The Hydrosphere; The Lithosphere* (Twenty-First Century, 2007).